CATCHISMS

CATECHISMS

Keith Howden

PENNILESS PRESS PUBLICATIONS
www.pennilesspress.co.uk

Published by
Penniless Press Publications April 2021

© Keith Howden

The author asserts his moral right to be identified as the author of the work. All rights reserved. No part of this publication may be reproduced, stored in a retrieval system or transmitted in any form or by any means, electronic, mechanical, photocopying, recording or otherwise, without the prior permission of the publishers.

ISBN 978-1-913144-27-2

Cover: by Keith Howden

CONTENTS

Incident on the Moor	5
Team Photographs	8
All my Dead Uncles	19
Monkey Business	26
Spiders	31
Pauper Grave	33
A Language for Stones	35
Cracked Mary's Holiday	39
Phyllis Dixey in Burnley 1959	44
For the Rector of Stiffkey	46
Faugh's Delph	50
Saltways Catechisms	51
First Electric Street Lighting	57
From: Landscapes with Handless Man	59
For Franc Sesec	64
Dynamo	66
Whit Monday	68
Cracked Mary's Mill	70
Memento Mori	73

Incident on the Moor

1. Joe Anderson

What witnesses? I call the ballock sun,
its banded light bounced from the canal fence
to testify. The randy cats sunning on
brown linoleum hold telling evidence.
Witnessing what? Joe Anderson among
his hunks of ripe and rotten meat to breed
maggots for fishing where, too long
confined, the particles explode
in iridescence, new bluebottles boom
and splinter in confusion at the light,
clouding the level sunshine of the room.
Do I subpoena witnesses to that?
Joe moved with a superb dexterity,
stalked bluebottles, cupping his hand
pelota-shape, to strike out suddenly
and hold them in his palm docile and stunned.
What witnesses? I call the willow-herb
raping the corrugated outhouse roof.
The cats at randy picnic in the yard,
if they had time, would offer certain proof.
Witnessing what? Dexterously he wound,
holding them unconscious and unbroken,
a hair about them. To the other end
he used to tie a small and banal slogan.
On summer days the layered air was hung
with his late captives and their droning weight.
Each hauled its trite but miracle drogue
through spaces of the still and even light.
Guinness is Good or Beer is Best was all
that he, Your Worship, managed in that sphere,
less sharp in mind than in that physical
talent he brought perfected from nowhere.
What witnesses? I call the ballock sun
to testify. I call the randy cats,
the raping willow-herb, Joe Anderson.
Dare I subpoena witnesses to that?

It was another climate and that sun
went black. The randy cats defected. Rusts
blighted the willow-herb. The bannered drone
of flies is hypothetical and wastes
in my mind's prairies. Joe Anderson
cancered and died. The defence rests.

2. Spring Song

Wakening spring's assault and psalter,
larks rang their bursting business of the fell,
plovers possessed a pulsing sun, the air
held singing distances for new growth's swell.
It was that day, crest piled on crest,
nascent earth's anthem for the spring,
with spearing tendrils of fine grass
and pent life driving, burgeoning.
The road, in the pulse of sun achieved
light's asphalt distances and realms of air,
married a trumpet light, the nuptial wind
swung rituals in aisles of looping wire.
That fullness burgeoned to a bleak excess.
A black discordancy, a breaking,
waited to breach the sun's largesse,
remap the contours of emergent spring.

3. Incident on the moor

Boys found, bird nesting on the April moor,
near where we lay, a hand-grenade.
Larks rose and fell. We heard the squeal of fear,
the dull explosion's echo. Someone 'Dead,'
was shouting on the ridge. And then, the men
returning with the body and the wastrel
soaring larks upthrust in spring's momen-
tum, charred moor grass stinking in my nostril.
Above us, suddenly where we lay,
black larks cascaded, climbing broken air
in flights unconsummated over the boy
with blown-off hands. And then that other,

that demon boy, white-legged, long-shorted howled
along the ridge. Larks black as time, but older,
fiercer than spring's explosion, held
his cry in scorn. Over the rim of the moor
we saw him lurch. 'Dead,' he was shouting.
Black-haired, he wore thick glasses and larks hung
black at his head, charred grass detonating
black at his feet. 'Dead,' he was shouting.

4. Love Song

It was that living day of the fell's grace,
the burst moor's celebration of the spring,
with spearing tendrils of fine grass,
a pent life nascent, burgeoning.
'Tell me about Joe Anderson,' she said.
I might have told the sun, its light
dancing in sibilants of acid
in half-litre beakers, the jewelled weight
of flies towing the miracle drogues
of Beer is Best and Guinness is Good.
I might have told the catalogues
of what she meant to me. I never did.
His hair was black, that demon boy. He wore
bottle-bottom glasses. Black larks hung
about his head and the charred moor
exploded at his feet. 'Dead,' he was shouting
I might have told the willow-herb's decay.
'Tell me about Joe Anderson,' she said.
I might have told the cats, maybe imply
that I loved her. I never did.

Team Photographs

1. Team Photographs

George led me to the wall where thirty one
photographs in black and white proposed
thirty one seasons of a side that never won
anything. Young and brash, we colonised
in callow ranks athletically transfixed,
a team without distinction. First, he stared,
not at myself but at Hugh Naylor, relaxed,
arms folded, head erect in an assured
self-confidence in some earlier team.
George spoke, voice loaded with reproach,
'You know the story, that man did me harm.'
He moved to point my later photograph -
'You're sitting where he sat' - struck visually
to shape our present quarrel. Seasons later, young,
I poised the same null landscape over me,
the slowly vitiating and corroding
townscapes of a time and mood less innocent
than I or our young faces had supposed.
Black and white stripes posed celluloid assent.
Petrified, agonistic, we advertised
different seasons of a side that never won
anything. Upland behind us were
the marches of a landscape I had known,
the blind and narrow town under the moor,
the pattern of the mean, ascending streets
that fashioned us. George pointed Naylor
and myself, wearing corrupting industries,
complicit in that landscape's weather.

2. Some metaphors for the Ground

From a turn in the road, the town lies
camping the moor's flank. Street fingers feel
and grope the fell. Chapel chimneys
tickle its thigh, the jugular canal
arteries through emptied mills. The decayed
white of asbestos stands unleagued
commemorates a side that specialised
in relegation. The pitch preens, grassed
to jewel, in the armpit of this dross
den under the moor. Chapels fail
in bids for re-election: factories
smoke on the transfer list where football
wears faces ripe to move from innocence
in seasons of a side that never won
anything, sliding a limbo dance
from league to league within its worn
tatter of terraces. Folded arms
and fossil grins commemorate a side
- hardened old pros in their last games
and aspirant lads, some of them on the road
to higher leagues - a schizophrenia
matched in results. The white asbestos
leans monument to lost sides that wear
thirty one seasons of a team that tows
its past to swell the grudge offence that sits
the streets and alleyways of this blind
tent under the moor where relegation waits
to stalk us in seasons not yet played.

3. Manager: Arthur Buckley

Manager: Arthur Buckley. It proclaimed
one of lifer's losers. Empty and likeable,
the world's fool, still my friend, unchanged
except his age and girth. He'd stayed the affable
man I remembered. The full-back features,
the swollen, heavy muscles of the neck,
retained their trademark. His body was
fuller but not much clumsier. He took

pride in old photographs damp had spoiled
with emulsion's bombs. Some were past teams,
some, action fragments scissored from old
newspapers, some gripped by blurred frames,
in postures fixing the naiveté
that held him gullible, the easy butt
of more worldly games. He could betray
my secret ridicules to grief, a target
making my blame ambiguous for one
of life's persistent losers. 'In this game
for twenty years, what have I ever won?
No medals. Never a cup.' I pitied him,
not his incompetence or lack of prizes,
but all he never knew, his dull goodness.
His world would need new rules and referees
for him to kiss its cups or wave its trophies.

4. Landlord of The World's End

Our meeting was deliberate enough,
myself and Naylor, near The World's End,
his newest strumpet, perching its fief
of moor and car-park. The accident
that scraped his wife to leglesslesss showed
no scratch on his surface. We climbed to
the moorhead. Beneath us, the town splayed
its legs in the offence of streets we knew,
that shaped simplicity within the space
our ignorance permitted. He spoke
derisively -'An arsehole of a place.
Alice told Agnes that you were back'-
then turned to gloat his World's End's wantonness
slutting the moor. 'It's mine. I always said
I'd have it. Something sodlike crushes' -
he pointed -'our sort down there. I made
certain of better.' Across the moor
his painted excrescence winked. I guessed
that there Agnes might cuddle the lure
of paper-back romances. Some malice paced
my own derision. 'How's Agnes been?'
'She talks about you, usually that night

dancing with you. She used to carry on.'
Despair or some once admiration might
have prompted him. He knew what I had tried.
'There's always Alice, can't be wasted'
- his equal irony brushed aside
my own - 'which of us is the bastard?'

5. Four sonnet conversations

i. Alice Buckley at The World's End

I knew the mock refinement of her voice
dismissing me as salesman when she said,
'He isn't here -' squawking her compromise
noises, not remembering me. 'Did
Hughie know you were coming? Are you new?'
The photograph behind her on the wall
was one I'd seen before. On it the row
of losing faces bubbled on a swell
of town and moor, a team on its way
to winning nothing. 'Mister Naylor's there -'
she pointed where he sat. 'He used to play
for England when he was a footballer.
He's out today.' She queened in his affairs
and thought she knew my business. I knew hers.

ii. Landlord of The Dog

'And so, you're back among us -' On his wall,
the serried photographs were spanning
thirty one seasons of a side that fell
steadily through the leagues. Shorts too long
and heavy boots were ranked in black and white,
shirts luminous under the hill.
He nodded to me. 'Hugh Naylor's got
The World's End now. Tarted it up to pull
the gin trade.' 'Does he get it?' He laughed.
My thought had been the vacant grey
of car park. 'Gets it alright,' he said.

'A bit more than he should, I've heard. Let's say,
visitors who might be better off
home with their husbands. Your sort of stuff.'

iii. Agnes Naylor at The World's End

'And as for Alice, couldn't you see
I've known about her playing his queen.
Couldn't you see I knew?' I saw that she
needed to tell me, had always been
ungulled. 'I'm not so foolish. I've known
about the others.' I looked for spite,
some spring of sourness in her and saw none.
'His little weakness.' Then I knew that
she hadn't been opponent of his games
but agent and entrepreneur and they
were gestures of a sort, her schemes
a kind of love, even compassion.
And then she struck. 'You got your ration.'

iv. Landlord of The Dog

On ruined and recorded landscapes, those
apocryphal photographs still wore
in agonistic, schizophrenic rows,
old disillusion or endeavour.
For his own ironies, he pointed
Buckley and Naylor, team-mates in a side
on the way down. 'You know he's resigned
today? Poor bloody Arthur,' he said.
'A job for Naylor?' Maliciously,
I fed the snippet to him, let him wind
his answer. 'He does one job for Buckley.
Greedy to give him the other.' And,
outside my irony and unaware,
he was still laughing. I'd had my share.

6. A rhetoric for Naylor's penitence

'I've had enough of Agnes. You can't tell
what I've put up with.' Scalding water
that he endured, I found unbearable.
'That whole bloody business with the car -'
He didn't finish or need to finish.
I knew about the car, but better,
its acid preludes. She danced to squash
her sour recriminations in my ear,
resentment fouling the night. Arthur
and Alice Buckley shared the table.
Someone took photographs. Naylor,
quarrelsome, drunk and incapable,
half-killed her on the way home, although
he stayed unscathed. She lost her legs. That was
the business with the car. 'I've had enough,
it's too much in the end.' In places
penance shower didn't reach, he raised
lather to conceal confessional.
'I want what going but can't get past
Agnes. It's left me with buggerall.
I never wanted more than my ration.
Just some sort of relief and mainly
what you're getting. Alleviation.
My life is skint.' That was his only
occasion of complaint, the one time
I saw the hurt sitting his centre,
in loquacious seconds when he came
clean in an assault of scalding water.

7. Those old photographs

'We've had them out. The albums. Old ones -'
Thirteen at table, a white cloth's furl,
a glaze of sharp magnesium hardens
apostle faces. 'Your red-haired girl –'
Buckley blinks central, haloed by an arch
of window, car headlights on the fell.
His palm lies upward, there is an ash-
tray, wafers and red wine. We smile,

in dresses and suits. Randy Agnes
fixing that flash in virgin white betrays
little except her smirk for Alice
at that strange supper. Her gesture stays.
Naylor leans near Buckley, his pose
mocks innocence. My red-headed girl,
now George's complaint, at that time knows
nothing, though my wafer lust was all
bursting for Agnes. By far the best-
looking, randy and available,
who, when we danced, salacious, promised
all that I wanted. Her tongue was full
of spite, jealousy and resentment
tricking her flesh's desire to splay
her readiness for a dance more urgent.
On the drive home, he scraped her legs away,
and that was that, our dancings undone.
All we proposed while smiling behind
the modelled cloth, the wafers and the wine,
the smoking ashtray, never happened.
Captured prophetic, Arthur Buckley
beams innocence where Hugh Naylor
postures the eternal judas-lie.
Alice smiles enigmatic, seems to stare
at truth on or beneath Agnes's dress.
'We've had them out. Old photographs that shame
you at your games. Touching up Agnes,
and that girl you shagged. What was her name?'

8. Housewarming

'No holy water with it?' I'd never known
Naylor to water whisky. 'Where's the tap?
I'm driving.' I recalled he'd driven
drunker. As children, we'd known the shape
of houses like this, were dough in these
unleavened alleys and knew the cages
of their yards, their rooms' geographies.
His water was charade to camouflage
words for my ear. We measured a bare
space of stone-flagged kitchen. 'Buckley's

finished. I don't know what they've told her.'
Our host's housewarm laughter cut across
his secret. 'If she knows,' - he eyed the regions
where Alice stood - 'she hasn't said. Cancer.'
Awed confessional and the kitchen's
cold air penanced it. 'Only a year
they give him. I hope he never knows.'
Which flesh or whose betrayal he ought
never to know I never knew. The brass
tap spun under his hand. Water spat,
rumbling piped to blur his confession
although he kept his glass an inch outside
its splutter. 'Some circumstances when
camouflage matters,' I think he said.

9. Apples for a dying man

'He loves to sit among his apple trees.'
Alice told spreading orchards to cheer
his illness. 'Out in his summer-house.'
Arthur was watching from his lawn's square
a match of wind and bloom. Six lean trees
were losing badly in an enclosure
of concrete, on that poor pitch, for his
last season's game. Fragile, immature
blossom was being kicked to defeat.
His hair had greyed, his cheeks sunk and thinned,
the bull-neck lost its force. He nodded at
the trees' flimsy bloom.' If you come round
a bit later, I'll give you some fruit.'
Wind butting urban sunshine culled
unfruiting seed. Sucking at bottled
stout for his health, he raised his glass to pour
badly, spilling liberal froth that rode
towards the trees. Bottle and flower
conflicted in his mood. 'Guinness is good.
What did I win but relegation?'
Seen from his shelter, the match had run
to its result. The bitter question
blew from his mouth, like the froth was borne
downwind to join the fallen bloom that,

once promising succulence, now lay
among the dead leaves and the birdshit,
latent to spur a richer life. Maybe.

10. A threnody for dancings done

'It's a long time since we were dancing'-
Agnes cadenced her tentative phrase
towards me, unsure but still causing,
as she had intended to cause,
recall of a time when we had had
hope of a different dancing as we danced.
That night she spent her venom in tirade
condemning Naylor. Now she evidenced
her need that I might still remember
our conspiracy. On the way home,
still angry, he broke the car and her.
It cost her her legs. That quarrelsome
night of our dancing brought back to me
her offers of a more urgent dancing,
recalled her acid mood and finally
her features, finely beautiful, parading
her crudest promises to my ear.
I searched new ironies for a face
once beautiful but now angular,
distorted and that night's ugly voice
the gentlest that I knew. She had been
urgent then, queer lewdness in her tone,
projecting it as her game's design.
And afterwards, as he drove her home,
that cruel, crippling business when
he broke the car and her. My thought hung
on the spaces of her life since then.
'It's a long time since we were dancing –'

11. Blackberry and apple pie

'He can have his home-grown apples with them –'
She poured the berries slowly and they ran
like blood in an enamelled sunstream,
pulsed liquid and uncurdled, from one

bag to another. 'Yes, it's cancer.'
Thin plastic squealed where her fingers fought.
'Blackberry and apple pie.' Her anger
held all malignant nature in garotte.
She screwed the neck, with deliberation
tightened it, to burst the berries' blood.
Ribbons of juice spurted a profusion
for vicious lubricant to her mood.
'With his own apples '- Jewelled sun lurched
on fruit debauched, bulging as she strained
to scorpion anger where she arched
and stung herself. Under her blenched hand,
swollen and tight, the red membrane burst
to spurt slush fruit. I heard her scream
of anger the distending bag released.
'What use are fucking blackberries to him –'

12. A fireplace with a copper hood

'Tell Naylor I know now.' A tongued fire
was blazing, brawling a copper throat.
His face, reflected, was a skull and wore
a medieval mask of death. A bright
scutter of ash moved firelight within
its indentations. His bitter words
swelled in a metal cheek's emblazon
on moquette. He slid dull eyes towards
team photographs, the lost sides askew
over the hooded fire, where in the line,
himself and Naylor grinned the same spew
of rotting stands. 'What did we ever win?
It's all a bloody cheat.' Firelight was
scraping a face ridged by the moquette's
impress. 'I know that now.' His braces
drooped slack to slip frail shoulders. His
trousers gaped where once his belly had
swollen the waist. A bluster of wind
was sucking elastic tongues renewed
from the flat fire. 'Tell Naylor I found
out in the end.' Which flesh and blood
treacheries he'd solved I never knew.

Such words he howled from that copper hood
were all time's relegations blowing through
poor sides unleagued shaping the bleak
metaphor of narrow streets, the sour
untruths of chapels, the god we make
from images of fear at what we are.

13. Requiem

Thirty one photographs still enshrine
those sides unfutured in their team rows,
screwing to private relegation.
Decaying asbestos stands enclose
the jewel pitch. Mills slouch degenerate
under the moor. Heads erect, arms folded,
agonistic, we commemorate
thirty one seasons of a limbo slide,
thirty one seasons of flesh and blood's
latent treacheries. Buckley's cheer,
if it survives, must simplify sides
in alien leagues. With Naylor,
I share ungrounded fixtures, played
away from home. More than the cameras'
coincidences fix us among greed
mills and chapels where our faces
stare into time not innocent from time
not innocent. We posture the bruised,
legitimate offspring of our noisome
camp on the moor, propose the crude
bible of matches lost in its streets,
acknowledge as our father the god
of games where relegation waits
to stalk us in seasons not yet played.

All my Dead Uncles

1.

'All Your dead Uncles.' Their images beamed,
Albert and Walter, James and John and Henry,
from sepia photographs unframed,
a cracked and yellowing rosary
fixed by shrivelled sellotape, forming
a rank on George's mirror. Puisieux and Serre.
Fell on the Somme. I knew the chiselling
of names in gilded stone: the year,
nineteen sixteen: a pigeon-woman's songs.
But better this, their soiled, immutable
immortality, their frozen starings
from the etched mirror, their suitable
patriotism. Bullet-belted, drawn
in khaki smiles and not that long from falling,
Albert and Henry, Walter, James and John
smiling with not much time for smiling.
'A hole big as an egg-cup in his head,
young Walter died in my arms.' George moved
in landscapes where his khaki youth had stayed
and my dead Uncles of his memory survived.
Water was running high. From George's, we
could hear the upstream rumble of the weir
marching its froth battalions endlessly
in regiments through the winter air.

2.

In George's house at the spluttering weir,
stuck to the mirror hanging at a lean,
Albert and Henry, James and John and Walter,
all my dead Uncles marched a garden scene
etched into glass. In a thin cartoon,
parasol girls kept eternal guard,
hollyhock lances speared a gilded sun
and in unlikely trees an unlikely bird
carolled a scratch. Two symmetrical
cellophane butterflies on suckers clung

to a reflecting sky. 'That mirror's all
I ever kept of what he left me. Young
Walter loved it. Look at it – a poem in
itself.' George boasted with no diffidence,
offering his aesthetic implication
as something I was sure to countenance.
The pigeon-woman's croon, the bloody Somme,
Walter and Henry, James and John and Albert
were emblems impotent to guard or damn
his mirror's mediocre tact and art.
The river wheeling woundedly and slow
carried detritus, scum making its march
in broken ranks. High water had bombed through
earlier, to storm the bridge's arch.
George dragged my childhood out of humdrum,
constructing khaki myths for my retrieve:
Puisieux, Serre, the trenches and the grim
mess of their ends. 'All bloody five
dead in a week. Young Walter looked like you.
Died in my arms.' In my mind's shambles,
George's mirror fossils their bravado
and permanence, all my dead Uncles.

3.

Cousin Tom's mimicry: 'Poor Walter died.
And Henry, Albert, John and James…'
With his thin face and frame, he imitated
George's stump walk and psalmodies.
Without a cap, he hinted George's, wore
invisibly the stained fag drooping slack
on George's lip. 'Piss Puisieux and Serre.
bugger his Somme.' Tom put his mark
on names I'd learned as rosary of a cult
more sensitive, the trench orison
that Tom, ungulled, heard only as the fault
in scratches of a broken gramophone.
Later, with George near the swollen river,
Albert and Henry, James, John, Walter all
marched broken between us. Tom's mirror
tainted their image, ordered our squall.

In George's garden by the weir, we quarrelled
where, at our side, sheathed leaves of lilac
strained to a disappointing spring. A cold
April morning saluted a fleck
of sun in grey sky. In the wet meadows
beyond the weir the weak light flared its sour
illumination and the white asbestos
of football stands was briefly golden. 'Your
sod of a cousin Tom's done this,' George said,
marshalling yet again John, James and Henry
Albert and young Walter, egg-cup holed,
all my dead Uncles marching khaki,
parading the river's swill downstream.
Above, the weir churned its April spate
in regiments of froth, their column
broken by mortar winds along the straight.

4.

'Caught anything?' George was loading
battles and blood into his query.
Wilf, oil-skinned, had caught George descending
to stall his fishing in the river bay.
Much comradeship involved the lower air.
'Wilf fought in France,' George said. I'd known.
We turned towards the splutter of the weir.
Wilf had progressed, was George's implication
into the dry, self-gratifying peace-
ful whims of age, while he had stayed to choose
politics' battleground. 'They call this place
Moscow because of me.' The empty phrase
cracked acres of time. I'd heard his same
expression years ago, a boastful paean
before the photographs and, mocking him,
Tom had stabbed accurately at his tone
and names I'd held as sentimental creed.
Later, I watched George posture, stand
by the rails of the weir as he proposed
himself, when young, dead Walter's friend -
He looked like you do now - Albert and James,
Henry and John, grey hair against grey sky.

Tom had been right to stab. 'They call this place
Moscow because of me.' My sympathy
for him had shrivelled. Puisieux and Serre
the pigeon-woman's songs, the Somme,
Albert and Henry, James and John and Walter:
George marshalled an appeal but it was time
to raise them in a morning's colder light.
'Caught anything?' I mocked his charlatan
postures with Wilf. Tom had been right
to stab. George spun deflated for me then.

5.

Fitful sun pecking the gilded grooves
of Puisieux and Serre, Fell on the Somme,
lit pigeons on the graveyard's drives
and the stump Cenotaph. Albert and John,
Henry, Walter, James: George traced the stone
East Lancashires. 'Young Walter looked
like you.' The pigeon-woman's croon
was with me but George had tracked
to nearer things. 'Tom Morton's made a mess.
One bloody woman and he's winded.
A pig's ear of a marriage.' Time to recognise
an old man anxious to be reminded
by any blandishment at my disposal
that he had stayed the four years of a war
and more than Tom had had his fill
of women. 'When we were over there
we didn't go without.' Scum platoons
formed ranks along the river's shelf,
swilled slowly down in punk battalions,
and open order, passing the Cenotaph,
the weir's conscripted infantry,
detritus bubbles parading in their
regiments on the move, a bladder army.
khaki impostures on the water.
'Apres la guerre finee
Soldiers Anglais partee,
Beaucoup M'amselles dans la family way.
Apres la guerre pitee.....'

I hawked the pigeon-woman's song and he
took it with savour. With it, I urged mistake
for flattery but offered a trenched mockery
without commitment. If he chose to look
no further than surface geography,
it gestured what he had wanted, lands
to conjure adulation. 'When you try,
you're the only one who understands.'
Sudden sunlight flecked the graves,
regilding momentarily his stone
East Lancashires, their fading names,
Albert and Henry, Walter James and John.

6.

The river marching slow in single shots,
grey water lapping the military weir,
attrition weather scorched the bankside flats,
trenching the waterline. A squad of star-
lings squabbled over bread. George lay
under the butterflies of Walter's mirror
necropolis, remaking loonily
his khaki myths. The pigeon-woman's wraith
crooned for him there, spilling the words
that carried for him the flux memory
of my dead Uncles, the bauble-lads
of Puisieux and Serre: Albert and Henry,
James and John, relentless as the scums
he told them: Walter who never died -
he looked like you do now - reclaimed his arms,
a hole big as en egg-cup in his head.
The river's sluggish channel paced his mind.
Stagnant detritus had overpiled
in spawny clumps. Capricious wind
flirted the clusters upstream. Then a shrivelled
and sudden, contorted anger marked
his mood. He jerked to mouth accusingly –
'Henry and Walter, James and John and Albert –'
marshalled their memory to damn me.
'I was your friend. Young Walter looked like you.
Tom Morton made us enemies, the bastard.'

Then sank to ride the river's sluggish flow
towards them, old and exhausted.

7.

In George's house by the spluttering weir,
stuck to his mirror, hanging at a lean,
six photographs. East Lancashire,
he'd written on each one. Crinoline
ladies, hollyhocks, that sharp bird among
the etched trees still commanded the frame
and of the khaki images that clung,
we carried out the last. Five chiselled names
I knew in polished stone, but knew this grander,
sepia deathlessness. Six cracked and faded
photographs had petrified a bland or
wondering, glazed but still unjaded
patriotism. Bullet-belted, shrined
in thin and khaki smiles, not far from falling,
unthinking, ignorant and blind,
five smiled with not much time for smiling.
The river sliding downstream, dully,
a light wind rippling in clearer patches,
cumbersome regiments of froth moved slowly
bridgeward, veered in gusts between the houses.
Bushed and intricate, contorted squads
slithered the river's central path,
swilled slowly downstream, punk armadas
under sunshine fading, past the Cenotaph.
I watched them drop the last of George away,
counted nine mourners, heard intoned,
with not much vigour, hope or urgency
words he rejected, watched them hymn the God
he'd never found. Earth that should have smacked
ritually at his coffin was a pinch
of finest to be found. With decency and tact
they killed what he had been. Judged to the inch,
we posted him respectably away.

I had mixed feelings for him then, played games
with hidden grief, added in mockery
another to those five chiselled names.

8.

On the stump Cenotaph's architectures
a generation too removed for pity
scrawled its bewilderments. Dead fusiliers
wore camouflage where obscene graffiti
saluted cruder loves and posturings
than theirs. From fluted pillars, pigeons
at their dung trades grouted the chisellings,
turning to shit my Uncles' gilded runes.
The weir in winter flood, its boom
built bubble monuments, toppling the spate
into a floodgate swill, landscaped a Somme
of scum exhaustion labouring the flat.
Daily and loonily she limped the rail
beside the Cenotaph, distributing
manna in pinches. Around her, a swell
of bucking pigeons scrummed to her song.
She threw a spray of crumbs, hauling a drogue
of hopelessness in her bewildered rave,
cursing the birds she fed, a monologue
that hymned her crazy no-man's land of love.
And there, beneath the Cenotaph, George spun
back in those silted chisellings that will
embalm and emblemise him better than
emotion for the men they name. Yet still,
let me recount them, all my dead Uncles, James,
Albert and Henry, John, Walter who died –
He looked like you do now – in George's arms,
a hole big as an egg-cup in his head.

Monkey Business

('Their witches sham death in delusion or delirium. This state, they call Walking in smoke and believe their souls fly from them to float the stars or rampage in some devil's satellite..')

1. At The World's End

Rufus, outlandish, platyrrhine swung
in a cage spanning a window bay,
a gymnast enclosed, performing
against a moorland spawning a grey
light clawing ravenous at the glass.
Lulled by a thermostat, supple limbs
played tropical against a foliage
of rushes and bare gritstone climbs.
Heretic heat one spidered night seduced
him to renegade. The moon's allure
garbled lost creeds of luxury and urged
escape to the cobwebbed continent of moor.
We found him mummified to gargoyle
within an overhang of shale and grit.
The famished inquisition of the fell
put to the question. Prehensile death
fixed the exotic leafage of his myth
in shrivelled contours. Spiders on the slope
membraned him, webbed him apostate,
stilled the dissent of an infertile hope.

2. Raptors

Fog thinly laminate on tarmac
broke at the car's buffet. The owl
dropped out of darkness in heraldic
headlong, a raptor's swoop to kill
its chrome reflection, a stuka strike
predatorial into the upthrust
belly of headlights. The famish beak
guided splayed talons through mist.
This was a death matadorial

in its short and ritual ferocity
and conflict of flesh and metal.
Only one bled. Above, a clean sky
diminished the whole affair.
Cold planets skidded a moonless vault.
Stars arched imperial to concur
such happenings as the universe's fault
where predators collided in a friction
of competing energies. They were
mere accidents of light and misdirection
made treacherous by chrome's mirror.
Machineries of flesh and metal's innocence
had found their absolute in predatory
collision, the raptor's necessary lance,
the pistons' robotic anarchy.

3. Double Vision

The World's End stood once nameless,
modest, whitewashed within the acid
greens of the fell. Once, in the arcades
of my young ignorance, it held
bright April sunshine, cloud shadow scudding
the reviving rumours of the moor,
scouring in knuckle outcrops, waking
the threadbare grasses. The World's End wore
my virgin landscapes, crowded the vault
bursting with larks. Gaunt poles ran,
quitting the road to file a thin assault
on the white walls. And then that burgeon
left me. Now, in darkness, bitten by
the headlights' mince, that once region
paraded a gilded whore, wantonly
scraping allure's diminished invitation.
Gaudy illumination spilt the name:
bulbs spat their bauble into mist.
Someone shouted 'Rufus'. At the time,
it meant nothing. Among the waste
of stars, one shuddering planet,
a clack of mindless laughter puncturing
the alien polish of the night.

I knew it then. Something was going wrong.

4. Cages

On the fell's flank, spirals of thin snow
balanced and spilled along the gullies.
That room shared with the bar below
Rufus's view. In her commodious
and like imprisonment, Agnes said,
'A long time since we were dancing.' She stirred,
leglessly reasserting what remained
of her once agile self. Open curtains bared
where blanched barrenness of the fell,
echoed our past's emptiness. Easy to guess
that double frisson and our once double
treacheries, our cages' invalidities.
I remembered her whole and beautiful,
cursing her husband and implacable,
it seemed then, to compound and seal
a time when we had danced together. 'Tell
Hughie,' she said, 'that Rufus frightens me.
I'd like that monkey gone. I know that he'll
listen to you.' But she had grown
sensitive in her crippled sentence there,
guessing me loth to try with real conviction.
Again, my lies were bringing back to her
the cages of the past. 'I'll do my best
Just as before, nothing would come of it.
It was a long time since we danced.
Tears touched her eyes reflecting white
snow trapped and whirling in gullies.
'I've been a lonely woman since –' Eyes were
dropped to the paperback romances
imprisoned, lying beneath my chair.

5. Walking in Smoke

i.

Something was going wrong. Once in the bar,
I walked in smoke. My universe evolved

odours of past deceits, another
moor's infidelities and in that broomride
an agaric otherness possessed me.
A night's mock Sabbat spawned the room,
gaudy and insincere on the witch upland,
wearing the fancy dress of beasts to assume
the prancing of animals. Nearer my mind,
irrational in its buzzing finery,
there came the bulging and prognathous
head of a bluebottle with plastic antennae
shivering my face to waken the mess
of Agnes's boudoir captivity.
Glitter paint shaped the leaning orbit
of multiple eyes. Within that stare
was the malevolence and the implicit
enmity of the basilisk. Fingers were
strumming the mesh of Rufus's prison.
Someone fiddled with the cage's lock,
'Give him his chance to join the fun -'
There was no fun. I walked in smoke
heard again Agnes's pleading, saw
through misted glass behind him,
our once deceits, a whirl of snow
twisting the landscapes of another frame.

ii.

Something was going wrong. Again
I walked in smoke. Again my cosmos
evolved the past's deceits, its coven
of broomride infidelities.
Again that agaric otherness
possessed me. My Beelzebub fly
had vanished. That Sabbat's gross
masquerading had left there only
some gaudy tokens of its existence.
The cage's lock was broken. I knelt
before its screech confessor. Rufus
heard mea culpas for promises unkept
and learned the carnal language
that Agnes and myself ingrained,

gibbering no absolution to assuage
atonement's need. Instead, he bit my hand.
It was his ambiguity to be held
both instrument and object of my promise.
A lost smock scarfing my hand, I hauled
doors from his stall and groped to squeeze
his space, to cassock him in the vesture
of that discarded cloth. Once more,
I walked in smoke, unfrocked him at the door,
to bundle his liberty into the moor.

6. Witches

Well, maybe Agnes. Disembodied litter
dressed the car park. A few animal
inventions and a mythic carnivore
grubbed among stones. My bluebottle
Beelzebub flapped antennae, octopus
on a stretched netting. Monstrosity
fluttered, wasting its once disguise
in bushes, its comic commodity
and plastic insincerity now useless,
already disintegrating. The world is
witchless enough and witches anyway,
were always fantasy. And maybe Agnes.
I saw the owl's body where it lay
and heard the land's language. Snow fell on
the inexplicable inscription
of stones: mist spoke the lost religion,
the old knowing. I felt the frisson
of a magic that queried reason's reaches
and groped to learn the planets' alchemies.
The world is witchless enough and witches
never more than fantasy. Or maybe Agnes.

Spiders

1. Monkey

We found that conscript monkey in a trench,
sprawled dead, his khaki battledress congealed,
where fallen trucks sheltered his sap advance
into the moorland's shale. A high command,
some inkling instinct of remembered liberty
ordered him breach his cage to march the moor
and soldier in that hostile territory
where trip-wire spiders waited for
the bayonet frost that took him stealthily.
We found him sprawled, a simple fusilier,
ignorant of who had been his enemy
or what the causes of the battle were.
Whatever trumpet called him, whatever drum,
they fibreglassed his mouth to fix him dumb.

2. At the Cenotaph

Our Lady of the Pigeons, to a sea-
surface of birds at the Cenotaph's base,
pinches her manna fine for agape
to spread among the spidered poppies.
Crumples her paper bag and grimaces,
twists tortoise head, spreads her arms straight.
Hands open demonstrate their emptiness.
Her late apostles now turn apostate.
All gone now, birdies. On that assumption,
a communal and multiplying flap
salutes her temporary crucifixion.
Crawling among the wreaths and crepe,
spiders might see what Cenotaphs afford:
the dream of something heading Heavenward

3. An ending

Iron and stone contending in the grab
and gouge of quarries wounding the moor
made backdrop to that ending. She tore a web,
complex and labyrinthine as our warfare,
its filaments patterning the cavities
of a wall's decay. Near us, gossamer
linked the rusting trucks. She broke their ties,
numerous as nerves, made metaphor,
in her destruction of their delicacy,
for our disease. Around us and between us,
wrecked membranes of the spiders' industry
told the fragility of webs. Such surgeries
of their transparent, intricate ligament
signalled the warp and weft of our complaint.

Pauper Grave

Eleven in one hole.
The slab's team-sheet texture
hides in deep grass.
Among the solvent graves
workmen are firing
the Corporation's leaves.
  George Musgrove,
  Dayman Derrick,
  Harry Dexter
were here selected
for an away fixture.

Some scratch and losing team.
Hard-fettled
professionals at the game
gave them no quarter.
Now smoke's applause
lifts from the leaves' smoulder.
  John Bridger,
  Wilfrid Widdowson,
  John Salkeld
are holding on
to positions in midfield.

The names tell one
of the crap and beaten gangs
of second-raters.
The proletarian, grey
syllables rune defeat.
The score is history.
  Sam Thompson,
  Albert Atkins,
  Joshua Hemmings,
out of the match,
trundle on different wings.

Workmen who piss
the steaming leaves contend
the game's improved since then.
Jack Blades and *Harold Knott*
make up a rotten side
whose cup luck brought
  disaster.
  Nothing here
  shows they found
supporters in
the crowd filling the ground.

A Language for stones

1. A Language for stones

Somewhyle with wormez he werrez and with wolves als,
Somewhyle with wodwos that woned in the knarrez.

This was a language for rough land.
Within its structures move the residues
of a more brutal world. An older rhetoric
asserts the echo rememberings
of a cruel supernatural.
Hard vowels trap the rituals of blows,
harsh consonants haunt with resonances
of the knapper's hand. Within its rhythms
exist the gestures of the primitive,
asserting fen and fell. Alliteration hauls
a syntax more of moor than meadow,
a grammar of rough transits outside the silk
civilities of assonance and rhyme.
The innate parables of its movement
acknowledge codes and hierarchies
of older and unforgiving gods.
It makes a direct stab into the senses
a word's sword leaving the page,
its onomatopoeic and alliterative assault
enclosing felt experience
in the first rituals of its making.
This language fights. Is a *knarre* sharper,
more threatening, harder than rock?
It carries an attachment to the thing
more energetic than aimless naming,
where sound and function are moulded,
propelled into the senses' world.
Faith moves in metaphors of rock:
such transits cannot exist in *knarrez*.

2. Before

Before speech
were the harmonies
of constellations, the impulse
swinging the galaxy's spheres.

Before speech
were the oratorios
of magma, the sun's hymn,
the moon's choreography.

Before speech
were the continents' rhythms.
the sea's orchestration
of geology's anthems.

Before speech
was the music of stone,
the constrained instruments
of a symphonic underground.

Before speech
was stone's imprisonment
of earth's locked descants,
its psalms waiting release.

Before speech
were the mineral adjustments,
the counterpoint of ores,
the songs of the knapper's hand.

3. A music for stones

Stone seeks its music. Manacled
in mortar, imprisoned in walls,
knows the direction of its longing:

remembering earth's orchestras,
the innate symphonies of land,
rings intuitive and stays

responsive to the hidden anthems
of its molten forming, to the psalm
continuity of its structures:
embodies the wet intricacies
and soft diameters of grass, the juice
hypotenuses of water's leach.
Within its caliper are the wind's hymns,
the latent animus and flex
of millennial seasons. Strike
and hear through geological time
the reverberations and assonances
of mildew's stellar mechanics,
of the seed's muscle, of the root's
slow hunger, rain's lisping appetites.

4. Runes

ab tells the moor's thigh,
black boulder muscled.
whose flex is seasons.

eb tells the vault's tears
whose fall from no face
speaks heaven's absence.

ib tells blood whose curdle
at the sun's bandage
grows the bones' wound.

ob tells the moor's eye
whose always staring
forbids the sun's escape.

ub tells flesh whose wound
by the sun's sickle
begets blood's boroughs.

bu tells the moor's thought
whose substance no substance,
whose icon is wind.

bo tells night's ball, earth's soul
whose silver scar in void
is skin's lost search.

bi tells day's ball, earth's rod
erect whose muscle plunge
and spurt bays increase.

be tells the bones hydraulic
palace and prison
whose prism is pain.

ba tells the cipher name
whose wound and sound
unsayable fuels the stars.

Cracked Mary's Holiday

1.

That summer, the wrecked Foudroyant
whaled on the beach, her rig awry,
her terraces of cannon cant,
I feared, to blast my holiday

God out of his sky. That summer.
under a shrieking seagull,
Mama's heels pecked the wet bladder
of strand. There was the rank smell

of donkeys and hot sand. Papa's
boozed baritone hurled What Are
the Wild Waves Saying? at the sea's
equal intemperance. Later,

in a shell's telephone, I
begged to be loved. Another
seagull dropped shrieking, a donkey
hee-hawed. The sea said, none to spare.

2.

That summer, I learned to fly,
rode the Big Wheel to value
a doll world under me.
Mama was the black sequin who

waved upwards, Papa the tipsy
tiddlywink. The greenhouse Winter
Gardens flashed sun. Epilepsy
twisted the world miniature.

Suspended, I learned flesh untoward.
Harsh kiss and impassioned hand
in the compartment corner ignored
a child. All they attained,

passions squeals and grunts, I made mine.
I ached to be loved. The wheel
wound landscapes up and down.
Level gulls roared, Not possible.

3.

That summer, the sham pavilions
on the pier's plank spewed flesh. So much
sweat and breath, like Resurrection's
pale millions blinking their retch

from earth, so much snot and skin,
a maggot's' dance, the mills' pupae
unearthed and wriggling in the sun.
Mama pouted headache. Papa

snored gin to his afternoon's
boredom. A few gulls shrieked for
gobbets. I posted sixpence
through boards to the sand under.

Eye to that slit, I watched them,
sprawled gropers in the pier's shadow.
I yearned for love but lust's drum
under me said, Not here, not now.

4.

That summer, to the Tower's
Longstone, I played Grace Darling,
at a polished sea pretended her water's
rodeo. An epsom salting

at the tide's crawl rim was my
lashed Farne. One gull's syllable
pumped my petrel and fulmar sky.
Mama I thought too stoical

at her rescue. Dear Papa
hiccupped at the benign swell,
tossed guts in a bored parabola
to that poised, hammering gull.

Papa bubbled vomit. A steamer
hooted. I craved love. A few
fish threshed in a box. Mama
said, Not for me, never for you.

5.

That summer, Mama said, No.
I, at Papa's insistence,
was hauled through new Meccano
lattices to the Tower's glans.

Sea had more weft than warp from there.
We gloated a diminished
and futile world together.
Then Papa jumped. I heard

his last hoot and saw him leave,
seagull spreadeagled in his last
drunkenness. He seemed to wave
goodbye. I had no tears. The rest

was newspapers' babel. They
dropped me between Meccano.
I dreamed of love. Reality
screaming the ground said, No.

Phyllis Dixey in Burnley 1959

Rituals deny surprise. What to expect
is on display. The ivory stalactites
of legs descend a drift of fur uplifted,
just concealing the bits that bulging butchers
will grope with eyes, debauch behind cold counters,
palp and possess in dreamland's orgies, rattling
their predatory tills. Giaconda Eve
smiles her long knowledge of the likely event.

Her monochrome portrait teases where Burnley's
tulips are squirting erect in April drizzle.
One breast, smooth and circular as a dartboard
poises its bull and inner on a froth of fur.
Tomorrow, the gallery's randy Goerings
weighing topside will coax its nipple taut.
She stands, Marilyn luminous, where the skin's
fascists are raising flesh's Nazi salute.

Rituals rarely surprise. The storm-troopers
of fumble fantasies are rallying to
their Nuremburg of tits. Stranded, she
seems a lost liner among the sweating tugs
of stale sensuality. Coy concealments
of chiffon flutter her *Aphrodite's* loins.
Butchers are howling their myth of a magic
and incorporeal meat. She lives outside.

She stands now almost naked, vulnerable
before them, in the daft trappings of half undress
but stays unreachably a dick's dance outside
their grubbing dream. Front-row Himmlers
rave her ritual. Black stockings process the aisles
of her thighs. Her suspenders glint crucifixes.
The Norman arches of her belt are colonnades
enclosing an altar. She is Mary serene.

Now the lecheries of grocers assault
the peeling dog-ear of pink sticking-plaster
legalising her crotch. On the mind's screen, she stands
dew-limbed as Venus on her shell. Gross lust
batters her tableau's bogus gentility
but something in the sumptuous flesh escapes
the air's bacterial and miasmic taint.
She seems innocent within innuendo.

Rituals mock surprise. She is different.
Something elusive populates the space
her thighs' parting allows. The ridiculous
is banished. She is now the sacrosanct truth
of slits and mounds. Even in prurient frills.
she sustains her myth. A cool morality
breathes her crevices. The Goebbels balcony
howls catcall propaganda. She eludes them.

Her breasts are sacraments, her nipples devout
as catechisms that the crap soldiery
of seats will never mumble. She is Mary,
Marilyn. Comes on the mind's screen, in Burnley,
in the drab fifties, this Eve before knowledge.
And not long afterwards, the insidious
religion of cancer groped her, invaded her,
tumbled her with the lust of a butcher's dream.

For the Rector of Stiffkey

Unfrocked for immorality in 1932: later evangelised from a barrel on Blackpool Promenade: killed by a lion while preaching from its cage in a funfair in Skegness.

1. To His Bishop, suggesting a truer Eucharist

Where mouths purse, your host is cash.
Your serpent rears to spit the oldest sin.
Mine makes a sacrament of flesh.
I damn the state's grocery of bread and wine.

My bread is dough of flesh to knead
in women's thighs. My wine is white.
My God, your bourgeois agape has unmade
God: my God, fervour and feast have quit

your celluloid ceremonies:
my God, you have table-mannered Christ.
But laying on of flesh outweighs
Baptism's mumble, the suburbs' Eucharist.

The subtlest mystery is flesh.
Metaphors don't transcend the physical
and mystics float concrete avenues. My splash
of truth incarnates the ineffable,

symbol and stuff of what we are.
I psalm the electric spasm,
Eden's blanc-mange, that blob metaphor
of immortality, the bones' ectoplasm.

I scorn your Altar's laundered, civil lie,
your Pulpit's social suavity.
My Eden anthems flesh. My apple
plumps for a subtler chalice's cavity.

2. Letters from Blackpool

Queen of my heart, my barrel,
as you might guess, grows harder, but suits me
fitter than faith. There is much to do here:
you would enjoy it. Glass *Winter Gardens,*
as relevant to winter as my former
Ministry to truth, spawn girls, and a wheel,
high as Ezekiel's, now spinning on cash,
tows poor souls Heavenward but always,
like Mother Church, drops them to earth.
The plump, skirted fruit of the *Gardens*
swells ripe for horticulture and the *Tower's*
varicose thrust reminds me of something...

Queen of my heart, my barrel
grows hard more often. Only my tongue
pierces the multitude. There is plenty
to see here: you would enjoy it. I play
between a fasting girl now spent and thin
as a Bishop's promise and a flea-circus
more instructive than religion.
Trams fixed and conceited as lawyers
pass the Public Lavatories where the sea wind
gropes among skirts. Fleas at their jumping
and the thin girl lying pale and exhausted
in the next booth remind me of something....

Queen of my heart, my barrel
torments me. The sea beats heavily here:
you would enjoy it. It does not thrust
slowly tumescent into creeks but heaves
frustratedly in and out upon
a beach where girls splay thighs on donkeys.
Only faces here are flint. Women,
poor foolish souls, jostle to touch me,
hoping I might confer fertility.

This mad sea threshing its buttocks of waves
into breached groynes and thighs apart nudging
the pommel's plunge remind me of something....

3. A Lion in Skegness

Now he hears his home sea. Only history
seems caged where the salt wastes of Lincolnshire
contend the sea's frontiers. Wind blusters,
a demagogue on the flats. All day the grass
shakes hand-grenades at the mud and panzer
cumulus manoeuvres the vault's corridors.
A storm sea roars habitual fascism.
This is a far cry from Stiffkey's Parsonage.
On its glittering estuary Boston's Stump
awaits the drone of Dorniers and Heinkels
in slow formation. Now, in pea-field and
long ploughland, Lincolnshire's Churches, steepled
magnificent as rockets, wait to obey
the Air-Marshal's ultimate command.

For a showman, not much of a pitch, but not
a cage. Skegness's windy sentry paddles
a spindle pier into the sombre levels
where time and sea running out deform
the losing light to a bleak propaganda
of coloured bulbs slung in a civil landscape.
It is a far cry from Stiffkey's Parsonage.
A newspaper with Spain for headline splutters
the bowling green's uneasy netherland
and recent rain has failed to wash away
the Blackshirts' lightning insignia striking
the seized garden clock. A sharp ear might detect
the radio's crackle and the dull drumbeat
of Europe on the horizon's other side.

More threatening and sinister than a cage,
these fun-fair girders in the declining light,
no place for a showman where the inmates
gape at the sideshows glowing ovens and hear
the screaming clientele of mad machines.
Swastika spars and gantries of the rides
plume tracers in a darkening air. The dodgems
contend and crash not far from the staccato
snipers and oiled weaponry of the booths.
It is a far cry from Stiffkey's Parsonage.
The zebra light and shade provide sufficient
uniform for the dispossessed. Another
train load will come to fill their vacant places,
to lose their shoes and win bewilderment.

Now he hears his home sea and here history
provides a cage and a sawdust continent,
a lion and a man. A few stuka gulls
are shrieking outside. Some in the audience
sense the sandfly time's momentousness. Here comes
sortilege in a skin. Stiffkey presages
Europe's slow tumble in this lecherous
and tiny actor. And here at the end of it
is the body's cage broken as France, the chest's
cavities exploded as Dresden, the ribs
ripped to Coventries and a belly butchered
as Dachau. It seems a far cry from Stiffkey's
Parsonage, this breath's broken economy,
the poor clown filleted by a mad lion.

Faugh's Delph

You are a learned woman?
I was never schooled. Some things
I have knowledge of. *The herbs?*
They have surprising powers.
*And this, you told the Court,
was where you met him?* Yes,
I told you, in Faugh's Delph.
Why there? I have no answer.
And what was his appearance?
He had no appearance. *What form
did he take? What shape of
familiar did he adopt? Was it
as a cat, a dog or perhaps
even a goat? Was he tailed?*
None of those. I have said
he was a presence, one that
I understood. *What name
did he have or give?* He had
no name. He has, as well you know,
a million names and they
are all the same. *And that
you believe?* That I believe.
I have no reason to lie.
His mere presence was in the form
of its own explanation.
An explanation of what?
His presence was the world
as it is the world, the world
continually and consistently
as we meet and endure it.
And that, you believe? I do.
I hold no evidence to tell me other.
You will be hanged. I will
be hanged. He told me so.

Saltways Catechisms

1.

Who names the moor?
 'I,' said the drover,
'In Bastard Clough, through Sod's Toll, at Hard Labour,
christen the salt's power.'

Who psalms the moor?
 'I,' said the curlew,
'At Love Clough, on Tolerance, over Sweet and Mellow,
chant the salt lanes below.'

Who pays the moor?
 'I,' said the drunkard,
'Through Swiggit, round Ale Corner, in Tosspot's Yard,
salt tickles the landlord.'

Who knows the moor?
 'I,' said the pony,
'Up Skidders' Bank, on Whip Hill, down Stumble Valley,
lugging the salt's economy.'

Who clothes the moor?
 'I,' said the grass,
'By Meadow Head, in Horsehold, under Goodshaws,
ripped by the salt's traverse.'

Who cheats the moor?
 'I,' said the shrine,
'At Jesus wept, at Mary's Chair, across Zion,
concealing salt's religion.'

Who shapes the moor?
 'I,' said the track,
'From Rake Head, over Slate Pits, at High Turnpike,
with salt wounding my back.'

Who sweeps the moor?
   'I,' said the rain,
'Down Foul Syke, down Deep Ditch, down Filthy Drain,
 salt to salt the waters run.'

Who shrives the moor?
   'I,' said the whip,
'From Jericho, round Hades, up Hell's Rip,
speaking salt's ownership.'

Who rules the moor?
   'I,' said money,
'Without me, Famine Ridge, Bleak House, Poverty,
salt worthless, the shrines empty.'

2.

I rant them, catechism,
those garble citadels of the moor,
names conjured in the prism
of a wry religion's grandeur.

Grime, Limers, Bullion:
Myrtle Earth, Rush Candle, Mean Hey:
Jericho, Noah, Zion,
Egypt: Slate Pits, Folly.

I name them, blackened bibles
of intake's apostasy,
assume their gibber syllables
in a rammel psalmody.

Ratten, Feist End, Gibbet:
Nouch, Lench, Gorple, Doal,
White Riding: Old Nick, Boggart:
Wormden, Bleakholt, Bone Hole.

I chant their dearth oblation,
the fossil babels of the fells
seized in their weather's incantation,
germane within their vowels

Nut Shaw, Delph Brink, Coppy:
Mary's Chair, Tolerance, Love Clough:
Horsehold, Whittle, White Kink, Cronkie,
Windy Gate, Rake Head, Nab Rough.

I tell their gabble rosary,
blab chapels of that plangent zeal,
intone their plainsong irony,
barren and evangelical.

Famine Ridge, Further, Windy Harbour,
Wreck Beds, Bleak House, Stone Crop:
Slack Myres, Wet Head: Hard Labour,
Needless, Poverty, Barley Top.

3.

They claimed the moor for neighbour, etched their farms
- *Rake Head, Windy Harbour* - in acid parishes
where vision led. Names gaunt with truth dissenting
the seasons' rituals, crude as wind ranting
its barren testaments. Faith's harbingers, they preached
labour's utilitarian religion.

Trespassed their neighbour's cloisters, sacked his shrines
- *Nut Shaw, Barley Top* - where they commanded
walls built to stem or swerve his sour recoil.
Syllables relevant as famine, each name
the thing it was, security against
the moor's revenges. They staked his land their own.

These were their lime evangelism's chapels
- *Stone Fold, Wet head* - faith's proper prisons,
sites christened by the land's austerity.
With pulpit vowels, hallelujah consonants,
denied the moor's religion, raised their psalms
apostate in their neighbour's mysteries.

Bibles of picks and ploughs, they consecrated
- *Old Barn, New Barn* - names nodding at hunger.
From laagered missions, won among the infidel
intake some scattered gestures of conversion.
Nothing recanted. No miracle redeemed
indigenous atheism in the grass.

The bald moor holds them now. The leper stations
- *Cronkie, White Riding* - where vision foundered,
stand sepulchres to that dead neighbourhood
gospelled in names. Nobody stayed. No labour
prospered to breach the moor's truth. Nothing appeased
a god dissolved in different sacraments.

4. Barley Top
i.

Came to the ruined, dry-walled farm
in one of the barren folds of the hill,
its rafters raking the wind, its barn
vanished, but on the spanning lintel, still

crudely but deeply chiselled was the name
I'd sought, the legend, *Barley Top*. It crooned
of my grandfathers' boyhoods, wasted time,
life undernourished on infertile ground.

Even now, though rushes and bog-tufts spread
and vaulted walls and dragged aside the door,
a different, limier green betrayed
land lost by and recaptured by the moor.

I thought of those old builders, the sour land
desolate, unpropitious to their hope.
The name declared an optimism and
sheep they must have kept, but *Barley Top*

spoke languages of pathos, the frail nimbus
of stillborn dream, and *Barley Top* broken,
crumbling at the moor's relentlessness,
was every foundered hope for me then.

Wind trapped and blundering among the stone
took me to times that solitary, wry,
my grandfathers acknowledged as their own,
shoeless before the turning century.

ii.

Brash in the moor's economy,
their outpost's arcane scrape
scratches a stone. Its irony
mocks their labour. *Barley Top.*

I wear that cipher name,
my witch emblem of the fells
where wind charnels a scheme
of supine stone. The lintel's

menhir mumbles the chisel's
runing, a wryness that honed
my father's father's parables
of hope dissolved in acid ground.

Now bog-cotton and rushes burn
its hearths, bracken panels the door,
lime's fossil taint runs stubborn
in intake garbled by the moor.

The name survives, its pathos
- faith's impotent contour
in the moor's relentlessness -
encodes their leper tenure.

Wind blundering the grass
conjures with bones. I mourn
my father's father, shoeless
under the century's turn.

First Electric Street Lighting

Working with Edison
taught him the trick. He said:
'Lord succour Thy invention.'
Garibaldi was dead.

Darwin kicked the bucket.
Grace abounded. Textiles fell.
He said, *'Heaven shall radiate
from Perseverance Mill.'*

Wagner snuffed it. He bottled
filaments of carbon,
specimen spiders and said
'God and Nature are one.'

Marx croaked. They dropped him
in Highgate. Gladstone
had his flies stitched and Hiram
Maxim perfected his gun.

He said, *'View favourably,
O Lord, Thy purblind son,'*
believing electricity
was revealed religion.

Huxley turned from his Bible.
He said, *'I will make night
and day indistinguishable
with ineffable light.'*

Kipling versed. He said, *'I will
hymn light's great Creator.'*
In Perseverance Mill
faith's humming generator

sparked. The Dreyfus affair
dragged on in France. He said,
*'Light steady and regular
shall colonise the world*

and man fulfil his destiny.'
Six filament coils
were his anthem. Hardy
planned *Tess of the D'Urbervilles*.

Gordon died in Khartoum.
There was gold in the Transvaal
and the dynamo's psalm
in Perseverance Mill.

He said, *'Darkness physical
and mental for ever destroyed,'*
from the steps of his mill
to the expectant crowd.

The Irish Question's rancour
loomed. He said, *'One further time
Thou hast made man master
of dark in his upward climb.'*

Somewhere in France, Pasteur
killed bugs. *'Let there be light,'*
intoned the Mayor.
Six bulbs brawled the night,

Simpletons on the fell,
at the throwing of that switch
in Perseverance Mill,
thought the valley bewitched.

At Branau-on-the-Inn,
shagging in the Custom House,
the wife said, *'If it's a son,
Adolf's the name I'll choose.'*

'Man is perfectible,'
he said. *'Hallowed be Thy name
for this, Thy miracle.'*
The Fire Engine came.

From : Landscapes with Handless Man

1. Gull

Slime paths we trod together. The river slices
through a steep turn, comes pumping a wet leather
over worn stone. Light's reflected order
shivered town's pulse. Over the water's thrust,
nightshift was clanging in new outcrop workings and
bulldozers ripped raw causeways in pale grasses,
fashioned bald ravage on the tortured land.

Jack jarred the gun to me. 'Young fool,' he said.
'This time or never.' I was unwilling
'Take it,' he said. I took it. We were quarrelling
over the river's shove. Then a trailing
squabble of gulls scraped over us. Tractors
were lumbering saurians coupling in mud,
lurching lamp-eyed in battered pastures.

Steam of thin mist was sweating laminate,
furring the river's throat. One gull swung wide,
rounding the water's arc. Puppet to all my crude
anger ununderstood against him, I
brought up his gun and shot. The hit bird folded
wings to itself. Mastodons in the outcrop dirt
blared barren challenges through the torn cold.

The shot bird plunged slack water, ripped the light,
set the whole river's banquet shuddering.
'Bloody young fool,' Jack said. The stuttering
tractors scored runes in a bald country,
searched starless frost with their headlights' flare.
'I've taught you better than that.' A long regret
was tearing me. He'd taught me better.

A latent anger lived in everything.
Jack wrenched his gun from me. The riddled bird
wrestled in faster water. Bulldozers reared,
predators at the chancrous land and ravenous for
its violated flesh. His mate dropped to him,

hung with him, spun with him in the sucking
water-race hauling his white wreck downstream.

She twisted mist-skeins over his bump riding
down a pace stretch. In turbulent reaches
hovered at combing stones. Her mate's race
bucked on the water's swell, swung sharply.
We lost him in foam countries, marked his stiff cruise
by her above, his eddying, sudden shifting
of ways with sticks through the mad shallows.

Tractors were famish dogs baying bald screes,
hunting the land in packs, pointing the spew
of anger riding between us. 'I'll never lend you
my gun again.' Jack's pain was spilling for
that penance bird. 'It's when I'm killed and gone
it comes with promises.' 'What promises?'
'Clear to you by the time you get the gun.'

2. Pit Accident

A bright day. Arthur said, 'Down on the floor
I saw his bloody hands.' Morning sun suckled
at chimney tits, drained a limp Guinness poster.
Bunched fists of cloud lay on the fell's counter.
'Two hands and nobody with them,' Arthur said.

Blown dandelions were spurting filament
parachutes, seeding the river's barren pasture.
A woman in a mustard coloured coat
dragged her snot child through sun in the street.
'Whose hands?' I'd always known whose hands they were.

'No accident,' Arthur said. Pale sunshine knifed.
In the allotment an old man's stoop attends
a sprawled dog with a bleeding foot beside
a broken frame. 'Jack Denison,' Arthur said,
carving the sunshine's trivial accidents.

'I didn't stir a limb,' he said. A black cat preened
on the yard wall, cocking a dietrich leg
suspenderless behind her ear and showed
a patchy undergut. Pink nipples plumped
pregnant to her coarse tongue's assuage.

'Struggling in the dark.' Across the pen,
girls in bright dresses flickered the paling
to dancing dioramas. The globe sun
bubbled bright gold. 'All the time struggling in
the bloody dark.' Our Lady's spire pricked nothing.

Children were plunging gravel at wet mud.
'Something you don't forget.' Boys balanced upright
on spoke-starved bicycles, their thin arms folded
to a proud handlessness. Sharp starlings banged
from roof to roof. Some things you don't forget.

3. Landscape with Handless Man

It is my mind's country, that dog's-coat smell
of stagnant river scummed and pooled beneath
a sky domed and oppressive as a skull.
Kaleidoscope allotments are jaundiced with

the year's decay. Ripe elderberries blood
the bankside pens. Swifts at their gathering business
cleave the far fell. Grey, captive cloud
clings, wool snagging wire, to the fell's screes,

teases to thinness, tears away. Now thunder
mutters. Time-lapsed, a second lightning stroke
shivers the water's pulse. Our Lady's spire
pricks nothing where greenhouse windows shake

timpani to the thunder's bass. A sough
of shifting pressures swells in pregnant trees.
Loose felting slaps tattoos in alleys of
allotment huts. Wind moves in swaying marches

through the bankside grass, draws swallows on
the river's pooling crust. This is my heart's
landscape. I know the eternal fashion
of bins and kennels inhabiting stagnant yards,

thin runes of aerials in a grey sky-fall.
I know the red bus on the hill road and swifts
gathering degenerate. These are all
changeless. In clock-ring patterns, tethered goats

champ an unyielding twitch. In the playground,
swings creak. There, among the broken rods
of sunflowers, the middle-shift compound
their garden platitudes. It is my blood's

country. In buttress terraces that screw
the river's wrist, cheap runners on brass rails
swing the spent greens of curtains soughing to
a suck and pull wind's pressures at the sill's

slit ventilation. White and ignorant
of the blear, spittle spark of thunder sun,
Jack Denison lies handless, buffets at
his bedclothes like a netted penguin.

4. He tells his love's landscapes

Here swill my heart's landscapes.
Clock dandelions spit their filament
symphonies in the yards. Swifts cleave the hill.
    Cloud on the counter fell
plunges. Loose feltings' timpani slaps
the long allotment's music. Wasps
forage and squander in the compost's rot.
    Sharp starling regiments rout fallen fruit.

Here sprout my blood's boroughs.
Grass seed in barren constellations sows
the river's restless firmament. Stone
    terraces plant my passion.

The red bus on the hanging hill-road furrows
my bones' infertile pasture. Black water mirrors
a bulb's pale onion. A smashed stool wallows.
    The cinder yards spawn brawling sparrows.

    Here blister my skin's passions.
Felled hay in hill-fields pastures her flesh's cry.
At the high lodgeside, disembowelled land
    bares itself, arches its wound
of unhealed outcrop. The steep overflow shrines
cascading water. Under its bastions,
ravished, bemused, beneath its tower, we lay.
    Swifts high and screaming pierce a bridal sky.

    Here spits my seed's process.
Mountain ash spill blood along the fell.
Freed water thunders over the lodge's lip.
    It was our Eden then, that deep
midgeridden gloom, that pooled sky, that rich sluice
bursting its business through a simple grass
in the deep hollow's wound, my green valley's fall.
    The white boat bearing me is a murdered gull.

    Here wasps my wound's legend.
Sunflowers' broken rods drip shrivelled grain.
She bred me spring and fall, my mallard pleasure,
    my autumn's flesh, my year
with its fat bellyful. She swelled my knackered land
of goats tethered on twitch, my hands' playground
of summer's squealing swings, that barren garden.
    Scrag bantams rut that parish's lost Eden.

    Here stings my truth's ruin.
Chrysanthemum heads are frosted hard as moons
in the midnight allotment. There has been
    falling and budding since. Once mine,
the clattering clockwork of arched heaven.
Was once a god. Once tore time's tawdry curtain.
Here rips my silly minute's fail and dance.
    Bursting my planet, here come the filthy swans.

For Franc Sesec

It was the last album page
of triangle stamps. Schoolroom histories
charted its ritual collisions
of Christendom with Islam, recounted
a Bosnia-Herzegovina somewhere between
grand-guignol and comic opera.
Not much prepares. A coaching Archduke
bursts in Sarajevo. Later, our wirelesses
tuned in to partisans, reprisals.
Newsreel flickered Stukas, Tito.

A tortured coastline breaks, confessing
argosies. Stone marshals mountains.
The sun's Gestapo flogs Dalmatia,
Montenegro. And simmering on
the roadside crucifixes, Christ is
suspended bleeding, somewhere between
sentiment and history, limestone
and blue sky. Ubiquitous as Tito,
the pillbox shrines explode in flowers
and plaster Virgins. *Not much prepares.*

Begunje: the white mansion poised
cool as a convent. There are a thousand
minor crucifixions of trapped flies
in webs mantling privet: a scored
history of walls surviving between
atrocity cells. A leaning triptych
of bullet-broken stakes still stands
to gospel Golgotha. *Not much prepares.*
Apples are speared on thorns and birdsong
stilled by the memory of eagles.

Rifle slung at his back, a soldier
is tying Franc Sesec to a tree. It is
another of those imperative
crucifixions, our century's face
and wound, this final dignity
in history's crumpled suit, that look
somewhere between martyrdom and victory.
Not much prepares. Woodland's renewal
wears no memory. The white convent's walls
immure the past. A photograph remains.

Iceberg horns of Alps are bayoneting
Slovenia's sky. *Not much prepares.*
A mason is grinding partisan names
into tank-trap monuments. Between
the gunfire rattle of his chisel
and Christ's wingspan agonies, Germans
play football. History here is blindfold
hostage to a tourist sun wasting
its shadows of stakes and wire across
the English faces crowding pavement bars.

Dynamo

The wind is in the east and icy.
It is six months since Hitler died,
five since the explosion
that scoured Hiroshima and three
since Attlee ousted Churchill. Droning blurred
in grey November, a Lend-Lease Dakota,
wings bannering the red star's sign,
steers into Northolt's landing area.

Thirty nine Russians dubiously descend
to the wet tarmac. Then the taciturn
interpreter that the press christens
Alexandra the Silent. An east wind
is blowing. Not long ago, Stalin
condemned Prokofiev for the formal
intricacy of his style. *'Do Russians
need sheets?'* is the question at the hotel.

For fourteen thousand pounds, Chelsea
sign Tommy Lawton. Five shilling tickets
tout for a fiver. The east wind's rain
soaks ration books in a bomb-scarred city.
A few journalists in grandstand seats
chatter dismissively, are unimpressed
by Russian training. Recently in
East Prussia, Solzhenitsyn was arrested.

Chelsea will sweep them off their feet.'
'Completely ordinary,' is the headline
in the Sunday Express. *'Don't expect poise
from factory hands. Lawton will get
a hatful.' 'Chelsea will easily maintain
our football supremacy'* avows
the People's columnist. *'These pale boys
are far too slow.'* An east wind still blows.

There is a collective gasp. The Russian
eleven shuffles from sweat suits and disports
the Dynamo colours. A dark blue strip
thrusts a pink D on breasts blustering in
a cold east wind. Their long blue shorts,
unusually, are bordered with white bands
and emerald green socks twist at the top
to white on these pale factory hands.

Worse seems to follow when each Russian
presents a large and colourful bouquet
to his opposite number. It has the scent
of dalliance, or worse, propitiation.
The crowd droops dumb at such unmanly
happenings, then gorges on chauvinist
gloatings and jeers. Only the sentient
see pennants flapping a cold wind from the east.

What happens is the unexpected:
inch-perfect passes from these hacks,
a new athleticism and such tactical
awareness, such spectacularly fluid
movement that leaves the English backs,
unused to such adroitness and precision,
looking bewildered. Stalin might well
condemn such intricate perfection.

Later, touring the blackened city,
they make their official visit to the grave
of Marx in Highgate and salute, though shopping's
still on the agenda. And eerily,
the rationed world feels less safe.
Sleet spits the tarmac where a plane,
a Dakota with red stars on its wings,
blurs out of Northolt. An east wind sets in.

Whit Monday

Listen: rearing into the hills
the road hymns release
from cramped terraces,
promising somewhere else.

It leans a Jacob's ladder
to scale the encroaching moor
where tankers, fonts sour
with acid, clatter under

the fell's scowl. Lorries altared
with quarrying's process rattle
the day's matins, haul
out of shadow, shuttle their trade

to different highways
where a changed prospect assembles
another landscape's walls
and different geographies.

Listen: the holiday's vehicles
of choirs traffic epistles
skirting the moor's oracles,
promising somewhere else.

Bladdering Whitsun's banners,
an infidel wind shudders
the flexible architectures
of Zion where whining gears

of hymns tell parables
contesting the sceptical contours.
A sermon's engine stutters
the road to eternity's bliss

and prayers broker a faith
alien to the moorhead's
agnosticism. The summit breeds
maps for belief's untruth.

Riding the landscape's quarrel,
the road makes manifest
different distances. Christ
inhabits the wind's swell

of blustering banners where
the tankers' daily religion
corrodes. The land's skin
is psalmed with acid, the moor

is yearly burned, the fells
daily quarried. The road's census
tells only its traffic's use,
promising nowhere else.

Cracked Mary's Mill

1.

They call me mad. My father's,
his father's father's mill this was.
Now mine. Brick broken fingers
crude for the sky's soft pieces
I watch through dolly-blue, false
curtain of my window-glass's stain,
cavorting children dance my walls.
Weeds reach to trip. I laugh in noon
green to the sun, stalk ruinous
garden's tangle, my father's
paths, my mother's luminous
borders blown. Convolvulus
is snakes, still parasol cow-
parsley cracks. Elderberries
flutter my hand's rape. Now
among mossed Morrises,
dead Papa's cars, and fungus
Fords, Mama's, I twine green
by the burst walls' bellies.
Was once their mill. Now mine

2.

Copperplate, indentured,
forty apprentice orphans
fevered within a week. Rye bread
so black and soft it clung the gums
like putty, sometimes porridge
sour and blue their foul diet.
Poor starvelings, before that rage
pestilence, death's appetite,
fell at their looms, committed
life on the cloth, were maimed by
senseless machines. Screaming died.
Saw horrid visions. Secretly
at night, my father's father,
his father fired to clean the stall,

pitch and tobacco to deter
the fever's rampage, had girls sprinkle
vinegar to cure the beds
of retching children. So much death,
rumour swears their shallow sheds
unconsecrated heave beneath
Fords and mossed Morrises
of my tumultuous soil.
Some say their bones crack in these
blenched towers of weed, straddle
their flesh through elders, bulge in
fat palms of hut-high nettles
as another century's pain
whose squalor forces the rank grass.

3.

I am the white flower's dance
in the night garden, twisting,
am moth and phosphorescence.
Am maiden silk trysting
with ghosts. Am seven veils bare.
My midnight garden riots
pregnant with phantoms. They are
here, those fevered unfortunates.
Fat worms have awled them. The gleam
belly of lodge butting the weir
quivers old anguish. I am
the cupped convolvulus flower.
In the stilled wheel's genital,
their screaming. My midnight's breed
cold flames in the crumbled wall.
I am the white petal freed.
More than the mousing cats, these
shadows cluster. One of them
loves me. His name is Peerless.

Among mossed Morrises in drum
landscapes we lie. He touches me
strangely. Oh, then the fine
champagnes of my body. Peerless
speaks secretly his passion.
I am my mill's Salome
at midnight nautches where,
damaged and exultant, I
dance the cracked flesh's grandeur.

Memento Mori

1.

'Not many like my voice but everyone hears
the message in the end. For you it might be
my sales-chat on your mobile touting time-shares
you can't resist in some uncharted country.
I hide in machines that speak your weight just as
your Mass assumes its capital. I inhabit
the lift's robot lips, the monotone that says
Your door is closing. You will hear my dialect,
waiting alone in some darkened station,
that blur from another platform's tannoy broaching
your ears with its message that the last train
to nowhere you can imagine is now approaching.'

2.

'Let Madam Sosostris nurse her cold in peace.
Forget her silly deck. Ignore her presence.
Your fortune is already told and there is
no chance that the shuffle and random occurrence
of cards can correspond to what you are
or what portends. In every horoscope
I am in the hand you are dealt and your future
is augured in my bones. So go and grope
your divination from some sad Sosostris:
you will pay her in vain. Whatever you do,
no matter how you try to play the ostrich,
I wait within you. I have always been you.'

3.

'I am the bone to which all other bones
have bent. I am plastic. My grammar is
I will. Words wear my terrorist explosives
and I have primed a fissile tongue to fuse
religions, to make gods and oppose them other.
I chew lexicons to put the slime behind
and melt the world's solid shape. My lips stutter
sin's documentaries, tell each episode
of salvation's soap. I scream outrage
in time's unhearing amphitheatre. *I will*.
Language within a world that lacks language
moulds me the Semtex architect of hell.'

www.ingramcontent.com/pod-product-compliance
Lightning Source LLC
Chambersburg PA
CBHW071410040426
42444CB00009B/2188